Harriet Tubman
and the
Underground Railroad

CHARACTERS

Tanya
a 10-year-old girl (in the present)

Gran
her grandmother (in the present)

John
a slave (in the past)

Mack
a slave (in the past)

Harriet Tubman
a former slave (in the past)

Thomas Garrett
an abolitionist (in the past)

SETTING

A kitchen, today; Maryland farm
and woods in 1860

Tanya: Gran, I need help. I have to give a speech in class about trains.

Gran: I don't know anything about trains.

Tanya: This one is called the Underground Railroad. I never heard of it.

Gran: Tanya, honey, I don't know anything about trains. But I do know about the Underground Railroad! It has nothing to do with trains that run on tracks.

Tanya: Then what kind of railroad is it?

Gran: The Underground Railroad was a secret way for slaves to get free. It went from the South to the North.

Tanya: People in the South had slaves during the Civil War. Back in the 1860s.

Gran: Even before then. And without the Underground Railroad, we might not be here today.

Tanya: What do you mean?

Gran: My great-grandpa John was a slave.

Tanya: I know that. It makes me sad to think about it.

Gran: Yes, it is sad. But did you know that John escaped from slavery?

Tanya: Wow! That must have been scary. How did he do it?

Gran: A great woman named Harriet Tubman helped. She took people to freedom on the Underground Railroad.

Tanya: That sounds like a good story for my speech. Tell me how it happened.

Gran: John lived on a farm in Maryland. His life was bad. Here is how my grandpa told the tale. . . .

John: I don't know how I can work today, brother. I hurt myself hauling hay all night.

Mack: We have to go, John. Crops need picking.

John: Forget the crops. Just for a day. We need a break.

Mack: Shush! The boss will hear you! I do not want to feel the end of a switch on my back anytime soon.

John: I was whipped once by the boss for not working fast enough. It hurt for days.

Mack: But I am bone tired.

John: Mack, do you ever think we could be free?

Mack: When I sleep, I dream about being free. But I don't know what it's like to be free. Who knows if I'm even dreaming it right?

John: Free. I like how that word feels in my mouth when I say it. Free.

Mack: I like how it sounds in my ears even more!

John: I think I know a way to find out how it really feels to be free. I hear that Harriet Tubman is coming to these parts. She can lead us to freedom.

Mack: Harriet Tubman? Wasn't she a slave around here?

John: Yes, right here in Maryland. But she got out. And now she helps other slaves become free.

Mack: Get out? How? If we get caught running away, we could die.

John: That is true. It is risky. But Harriet Tubman knows people between here and Canada who can help. They believe in freedom for all people. They move and hide runaway slaves.

Tanya: Is that what they did, Gran? Wasn't it dangerous?

Gran: Yes! Any slave who made it to a free state up north could be sent back south. To really be free, you had to go to Canada.

Tanya: It's a long way from Maryland to Canada!

Gran: It sure is far. And they walked most of the way. But Harriet Tubman was smart. She did the trip many times.

Tanya: She never got caught?

Gran: No. She had secret ways of sending messages. For example, she used songs to tell the slaves when to go and what to do. One song went like this . . .

Harriet *(sings)*: "When the sun comes back and the first quail calls, follow the drinking gourd.
For the old man is waiting for to carry you to freedom,
if you follow the drinking gourd."

John: Mack, hear that song Harriet is singing? "When the sun comes back ..." That means when winter ends and spring begins. That's when we leave.

Mack: I get it. And "the drinking gourd" is the Big Dipper, the stars we see in the night sky. The ladle points to the North Star.

John: We follow that star to go North, to freedom.

Gran: John and Mack went North. Harriet Tubman led the way.

Harriet: Along the way, there are safe houses. People help with food and shelter.

Mack: At every stop?

Harriet: No, Mack. Sometimes, we hide ourselves. I know good places.

John: I've never walked so far or so fast. My shoes are in tatters.

Harriet: In two nights' time, we will stop at the shoe shop of Tom Garrett. He is a good man, a friend.

John: Mack and I are a little scared. Are you sure we won't be found?

Harriet: I never ran my train off the track, and I never lost a passenger. Keep going.

Gran: They walked for days. They went through rivers. They hid in barns. Finally, they made it to the shoe shop.

Garrett: Harriet! You are finally here. Bad news. There's a sign in town—"Runaway slaves." It may be your men they are talking about.

Harriet: My men are hiding in the woods. I'll warn them.

Garrett: We must be quick. I hired a cart to bring you to your next stop.

Harriet: You are a good man, Tom Garrett. You are truly blind to a person's color.

Garrett: I see past a person's skin to the goodness inside. Now, they are two big men, you say? Try these shoes. The cart will wait by the stream.

Gran: Harriet went back to John and Mack. She sang as she walked.

Harriet: (*sings quietly*) "Go down, Moses, way down in Egypt land. . . ."

Mack: "Go down, Moses . . ." That means it's time to move on.

Harriet: Hush. White men are looking for you. They will get $200 if they find you.

Mack: We'll get caught!

Harriet: No, you won't. Now follow me to the stream. This cart here will take you to the next stop on the Underground Railroad. You must hide under the bricks.

John: Okay, Harriet. But under all these bricks, I feel like I'm in a coffin.

Mack: I can hardly breathe.

John: Take it slow, Mack. Soon you will be tasting the sweet air of freedom.

Harriet: That is right. We got to go free or die. Now, move on, cart!

Tanya: Did they make it, Gran?

Gran: We are here today, are we not? John and Mack made it to Canada. After the slaves were set free, they moved to New York. They got married. They had children.

Tanya: Including your grandpa! How many people did Harriet Tubman bring along the Underground Railroad?

Gran: About 300. On at least eighteen different trips.

Tanya: Wow! She risked her life all those times. What a hero! I think I have my speech.

Gran: John would be proud.

The End